Face-to-Face
NIGHT CREATURES

What's Inside?

When Night Falls

At night, many animals snuggle down to sleep while others are just waking up, ready for breakfast. The night is a safe time to hunt for food because enemies are often fast asleep! There are all kinds of night creatures, from spooky owls to howling wolves and tiny insects. Let's meet a few.

An emperor moth smells his mate and flies off to find her.

A ghostly owl hoots loudly to warn other owls to keep away.

WoW!
Most night animals can see in the dark, but they can't see colors. To them, everything is black and white!

Bats open their huge, leathery wings and swoop through the sky.

A leopard creeps out of the bushes, on the lookout for a snack.

3

Bats

There are hundreds of different kinds of bats. They live all over the world except in very cold places. All bats have furry bodies and long, leathery wings. During the day, huge groups of bats doze upside down in caves or treetops. At dusk, they wake up and go hunting.

Q Are bats blind?

A No! Bats aren't blind, but most can't see well. They can see about as far as you can in the dark.

Now I really can't see anything!

Some bats love to munch on insects while others adore juicy tropical fruits. A few bats eat frogs, fish, and even other bats!

Bats make noises to help them fly to the right place. The noises bounce off objects, such as trees, and come back to the bat. This tells the bat where the trees are.

The world's smallest bat is called a Kitti's hog-nosed bat. It's so tiny it could easily fit inside a matchbox!

Listen Up!

Night creatures make all kinds of noises, from sweet songs and ringing chirps to spooky howls. It's their way of talking to one another. Sometimes, the animals are calling out for a friend. At other times, they're saying, "Don't come near me!"

▼ Frog Chorus

In spring, male bullfrogs sing to attract mates. Each male puffs out his throat so it looks like a giant bubble. The female bullfrogs hop closer to listen.

◀ Beware

Wolves live in groups called *packs*. When one wolf howls, the other pack members join in. The noise can be heard for miles around and warns other wolves to stay away.

WOW!
If you were at the front of a long train, you'd be able to hear a bush cricket's chirp at the back of the train!

Can You Believe It?

A hyena's call sounds like loud, shrieking laughter! When other hyenas hear it, they know that food is nearby and race to share the feast.

Dinner! Ha-ha-haa!

▶ What a Noise!

On warm evenings, male crickets chirp noisily in fields. This tells female crickets where they are. A cricket sings by rubbing its two front wings together.

7

Bushbabies

A bushbaby's enormous eyes and flapping ears help it to find creepy crawlers in the dark. The bushbaby sits quietly in a tree and grabs tasty insects out of the air with its fingers. It also feasts on small mice, lizards, fruits, and leaves.

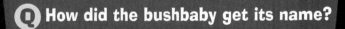
Q How did the bushbaby get its name?

A A bushbaby lives in parts of Africa called the "bush" and when it calls out, it sounds just like a crying baby!
Now put the words *bush* and *baby* together!

It's a Laugh!
Which snake does a bushbaby like to play with?
A rattle-snake!

Bushbabies are great acrobats. They jump from tree to tree so quickly that hardly anything can catch them.

A bushbaby has a sharp claw on one of its toes, used especially for scratching the back of its neck and cleaning out its ears.

As soon as a bushbaby is born, it goes on a piggyback ride! The tiny baby clings safely to its mother's back while she hunts for tasty insects and juicy fruit to eat.

Keeping Alert

Night creatures have special ways of dealing with the dark. Many have a fantastic sense of smell and supersharp hearing. These amazing senses help them to find food and stay out of danger. A few animals can see better in the dark than you can in the daytime.

Can You Believe It?

A female emperor moth makes herself smelly to find a perfect mate. She gives off a special odor that a male moth can sniff from several miles away.

Hang on. I'm coming!

◀ I Can Hear You!

An aye-aye's huge ears are perfect for tracking down its favorite meal. It can easily hear tiny beetle grubs munching wood inside a rain forest tree branch.

WOW!

A tiny insect called a cicada can hear up to 100 different sounds in one second!

▶ Eye Spy

You can't sneak up on a tarsier in the rain forest. Not only does it have huge eyes, but it can also swivel its head around to see backward!

◀ Sniffing for a Snack

A kiwi spends the night prodding the forest floor with its long, flexible bill. This bird, which cannot fly, has nostrils at the tip of its bill for sniffing out worms and insects.

Leopards

Leopards are large cats that live in jungles, mountains, and forests. During the day, they lounge around in trees. But leopards are also fierce hunters. In the dead of night, a leopard creeps up on its prey, then leaps and grabs the unlucky animal with its front paws.

It's a Laugh!
Why don't leopards play hide-and-seek? Because they're usually spotted!

Q Do all leopards have spots?

A Yes, but you can't always see them! A few leopards are born with dark fur that hides the spots. These leopards are called black panthers.

Where did my spots go?

A hungry leopard isn't a fussy eater. It will even gobble down a spiky porcupine when it is hungry.

A clouded leopard can hang from a branch by one paw while it grabs at a passing snack with another paw.

Sometimes a leopard hunts by jumping around in a tree to make it shake. When a baboon slips and falls to the ground, it's dinnertime!

Night Hunters

At night, hungry hunters lurk in the shadows, ready to pounce on passersby. The night can be a dangerous time for juicy insects and other small creatures. A bold beast might even creep up on a sleeping creature and give it a sudden wake-up call!

▶ Fishy Treat

Can you imagine fishing in the dark? It's a raccoon's favorite hobby! A raccoon catches a fish with its front paws and may even flick it out of the water!

▼ Park Raid

When you're fast asleep, foxes are on the prowl. They catch mice and small birds, and sometimes even eat the leftovers in trash cans!

WOW! One little brown bat can catch and eat up to 1,200 insects in an hour!

Can You Believe It?

A giant anteater's sticky tongue is longer than your leg! The tremendous tongue is perfect for licking up tons of ants or even a tasty ice-cream cone!

Keep off!

▶ Ocean Nibbler

A moray eel is a deadly ocean hunter with a superb sense of smell. The eel sniffs out fish in a coral reef, then crunches them with its jagged teeth.

Owls

An owl hunts mainly at night, using its large eyes and keen ears to find food on the ground. It opens its mighty wings, swoops silently through the sky, then dives on its prey. A small animal, such as a rabbit, has no chance against the owl's long, sharp claws and hooked beak.

Q **Does an owl have eyes in the back of its head?**

A Almost! An owl can turn its head completely around to face backward. If a creature creeps up behind an owl, the owl just swivels its head and catches it in the act!

An owl gulps down small animals such as voles and mice whole. Later, it coughs up little pellets made of their fur and bones.

You wouldn't want a great horned owl as an enemy! This fearsome hunter snaps up barn owls and even smelly skunks.

A screech owl makes strange hoots telling you to keep away from its nest. In the past, people thought the spooky noises warned of disaster.

Glow in the Dark

A few amazing creatures glow brightly in the dark by making light inside their bodies. On land, glowworms twinkle against the night sky like tiny stars. In the dark ocean, fierce fish hunt by the light of their gleaming bodies.

Can You Believe It?

A railroad worm has a shock in store for its enemies. The creature's head shines bright red and its body glows yellow to scare off attackers.

Watch Out!

In the deep murky ocean, an anglerfish plays a nasty trick. It dangles its glowing fin like a fishing rod. When tiny fish come to look, the hunter gobbles them up.

▼ Lighting Up

When a female glowworm wants a mate, she switches on a light at the end of her body. A passing male spots the friendly glow and zooms down to visit.

▼ Which Way Now?

A flashlight fish has a bright patch of light under its eyes. When night falls, this special lantern comes in handy for finding food on a coral reef.

WOW!

The beam from a flashlight fish is so bright that it can easily light up a small room!

Puzzle Time

Here are a few puzzles to try. You can look back in the book to help you find the answers.

True or False?

How much do you know about night animals? Answer these true or false questions to find out.

1 A few bats eat fish. Hint: Go to page 5.

2 When a bushbaby is born, it rides around on its father's back. Hint: Go to page 9.

3 Leopards are fussy eaters. Hint: Go to page 13.

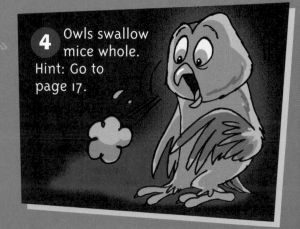

4 Owls swallow mice whole. Hint: Go to page 17.

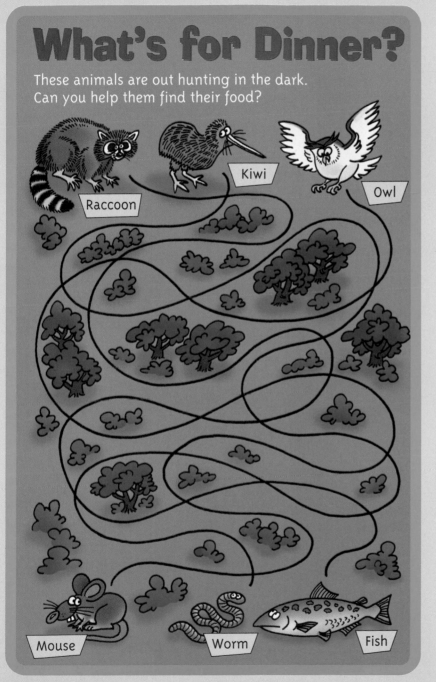

What's for Dinner?

These animals are out hunting in the dark.
Can you help them find their food?

Raccoon

Kiwi

Owl

Mouse

Worm

Fish

Close-up

We've zoomed in on these night creatures. Can you name them?

1 Hint: Go to page 3.

2 Hint: Go to page 6.

3 Hint: Go to page II.

Index

Created by act-two for Scholastic Inc.
Copyright © act-two, 2001.
All rights reserved. Published by Scholastic Inc.
SCHOLASTIC and associated logos are trademarks
and/or registered trademarks of Scholastic Inc.

Main illustrations: Eric Robson
Cartoon illustrations: All cartoon illustrations by Simon Clare
except for pp. 20-21 Geo Parkin, p. 23 Alan Rowe
Consultant: Barbara Taylor
Photographs: cover Bruce Coleman Inc., pp. 4-5 Bruce Coleman Inc.,
pp. 8-9 NHPA/Stephen Dalton, pp. 12-13 Corbis UK/Chase Swift,
pp. 16-17 FLPA/S. Maslowski

ISBN 0-439-31711-8

12 11 10 9 8 7 6 5 4 3 2   2 3 4 5 6/0

Printed in the U.S.A.

First Scholastic printing, September 2001